College Slang 101

A definitive guide to words, phrases and meanings they don't teach in English class

"Hark the sound of Tarheel voices
Ringing clear and true . . ."

For the many Tarheel voices
who have contributed to this collection.

The students of
English 36 and English 94A
1972-1989

College Slang 101

BY CONNIE EBLE

ILLUSTRATIONS BY FELIPE GALINDO

Art Direction and Design • Anthony LaSala
Production • Akiko Taniyama
• Takahiro Yamatsu

Published by Spectacle Lane Press

About the Author

It would seem that a college professor of English would abhor slang and forever ban it from the classroom.

But this is not the case with the author of *College Slang 101,* Connie Eble, an associate professor who has taught English at the University of North Carolina at Chapel Hill since 1971.

Not only does she recognize slang for its social values and the enriching effect it can have on the English language, but she has devoted a considerable amount of time and effort to its study.

Connie Eble

An authority on the group-identifying language of American college students, Connie Eble holds a master's degree and a doctorate in linguistics from the University of North Carolina and is active in such organizations as the Linguistic Association of Canada and the United States, the American Dialect Society, and the Modern Language Association.

She has done extensive research into the development of the English language and has authored numerous articles, reviews and conference papers in her specialty.

She became interested in college slang when she began using it as a teaching aid to make English grammar more palatable for her students.

What began as a means to an end became an end in itself, not only for Connie Eble but for her students who, over the years, have helped her gather the hundreds of examples of college slang that make up the unique collection presented for the first time in this book.

Photo by Loy C. Smith

College Slang 101

CONTENTS

CONTENTS

CONTENTS

Social Donut

College Slang 101

I. The Nature of College Slang
A Microcosm of Language

Despite what many of its trendiest contemporary users may believe, college slang is as old as colleges and universities themselves.

Ever since the Middle Ages, when young men left the supervision of their families and flocked to such centers of learning as Paris and Bologna to pursue learning and life in a community of scholars, students have created an ever-changing set of words and phrases to strengthen their group identity and to set themselves off from others.

Perhaps the earliest recorded example of student slang is preserved from those early university years when scholars appeared for tutelage in long black robes and hoods and were expected to converse at all times in Latin. This early slang term is *lupi*, the Latin word for "wolves." It referred to "spies who reported students for using the vernacular instead of Latin."

A Vocabulary for Grumbling

Undoubtedly, the same scholars that failed to apply themselves assiduously to the mastery of Latin and complained about the *lupi* also developed a vocabulary to grumble about the unreasonable expectations of their teachers, the quality of the food, the effects of drinking too much, and other time-honored student preoccupations. However, because of the oral and ephemeral nature of slang, that vocabulary has been lost to us forever.

College Slang 101 is based on a vocabulary identified with quite a different breed of students — undergraduates of American colleges and particularly those enrolled in

11

a large, Southern state university during the 1970's and 1980's. The hundreds of words and phrases of college slang in this book are all examples reported to me by students enrolled in English 36 and English 94A at the University of North Carolina at Chapel Hill between fall of 1972 and spring of 1989.

Accelerated Rate of Change

The collection from which the examples in *College Slang 101* have been drawn spans a period of seventeen years. Like the general vocabulary, slang changes constantly. But by comparison with vocabulary change in the language as a whole, which sometimes takes centuries, the rate of change in slang vocabularies is greatly accelerated. Only four items reported as good, campus slang in 1972 were reported in use with the same meanings in 1989: *bad* (good); *bummer* (an unpleasant experience); *slide* (an easy course); and *wheels* (car). For some inexplicable reason, these four appear to have staying power, like the slang word *booze*, which dates from at least the time of Chaucer.

Because of the complexities involved, dates are not given in this book for the individual slang items. Some, like many of the synonyms for *drunk*, have been part of the informal vocabulary of English for centuries and get taken up for short periods by college students. For example, *cut the rug* (to dance) from the 1930's was resurrected in 1978 and 1979 but is once more out of use.

Other slang terms seem to die, only to show up a few years later with a different meaning. Thus *cheeseman* in the spring of 1979 referred to a male who pursued women, i.e., who went after *cheesecake*. In the spring of 1989 the term *cheeseman* has been recreated to refer to "a male who is unpleasant, i.e., *cheezy*." Words that meant *drunk* prior to the 1960's were shifted to refer to "the effects of drugs," like *stoned*. Several of them are now in use again to mean *drunk.* All of the slang items in *College Slang 101* were in use with the meanings given sometime between 1972 and 1989.

Sources of Slang

Slang provides a microcosm of language. The many ordinary word-forming processes at work in the production of slang are shown in the chapter "The Origins of College Slang." Many slang words are affected by more than one process, and a few words in this book appear in more than one category. *Waste product* (a drunk), for example, could illustrate three categories: it is a compound and a metaphor and draws on an image of destruction to depict intoxication.

In addition, once a slang word is established, it tends to acquire quickly a set of grammatically related forms. Thus *freak out* shows up in the forms *freak, freaks, freaking, freaked, freaky, freaker. Space out, trip out,* and many others show the same generative pattern.

Very few of the slang items in *College Slang 101* were actually created on the University of North Carolina at Chapel Hill campus, and most were in use at a wide variety of colleges and universities across the country at roughly the same time. Many are recognizable as belonging to the highly informal level of general American English, like *blast* (party); *burned out* (exhausted); *cool* (stylish); *Mickey Mouse* (easy); *nerd* (unlikable, socially inept person); *psyched* (mentally prepared); and *uptight* (nervous). Some originated in other subcultures and have been adopted by college students, like *tubular* (excellent) from surfing and *jamming* (playing music and dancing) from the language of Black musicians.

Slang is Oral

Slang is oral. The transmission of slang by word of mouth guarantees some shift of meaning or distortion of sound as the network of users of a particular expression increases. For example, words that enter the language as coarse and vulgar expressions with a sexual referent sometimes retain their negative force while losing the specific reference to sex, like *grease* (eat) and *screw* and *hose* (to treat unfairly). Often the original meaning is retained alongside the newer, less offensive sense, and context and tone of voice allow the hearer to decide which meaning is intended. Phonetic distortion has altered, for example, the expression *crip course* (easy course), from a course for *cripples,* to *crib course*, which makes equally good sense.

Linguistic Equivalent of Fashion

The aim of using slang is seldom the exchange of new information. College students use slang to identify with each other or with a trend or fashion. Their constantly changing slang vocabulary is the linguistic equivalent of fashion and serves much the same purpose. Like stylish clothing and modes of popular entertainment, effective slang must be new, appealing, and able to gain acceptance in a group quickly. Nothing is more damaging to status in the group than using old slang.

The psychological security of a shared slang vocabulary during the college years should not be underestimated. Slang allows college students to endure and enjoy together that twilight zone between adolescence and adulthood. No arbitrary rules in grammar books make slang items right or wrong, and for the most part current slang cannot even be found in a dictionary. Thus their slang allows college students the freedom to have fun with the language; to make words up; to adopt new expressions indiscriminately; and to use language for humor, irony, sarcasm, and irreverence.

Connie Eble
University of North Carolina
Chapel Hill, North Carolina

College Slang 101

II. The Origins of College Slang:
Recycling Old Words

Slang items usually arise by the same means in which new words enter the general vocabulary — by recycling words and parts of words which are already in the language. In the recycling process either the shape or the sense of a word, or both, can be altered to yield a new and different union between sound and meaning. This is the way that standard English has recently added words like *AIDS* (acquired immune deficiency syndrome), *fax* (to transmit a facsimile electronically over telephone lines), and *microwave* (to cook by heat produced by short electromagnetic waves).

By the same kinds of processes, slang has created *TAN* (tough as nails), *preesh* (appreciate), and *megabread* (large amount of money). This chapter shows the various productive processes that give rise to college slang.

SLANGDOM:
Adding Prefixes and Suffixes

Ordinary English uses prefixes and suffixes to make new words. *Prearrange, predate,* and *pretrial* are made by adding the prefix *pre-* to different words. The suffix *-er,* which means "one who or that which," turns a verb into a noun in words like *dancer, joker, player,* and *singer.* Slang uses many of the same prefixes and suffixes as ordinary English but sometimes with greater freedom and slightly different meanings or grammatical functions.

MEGA- A large quantity of: *megabitch, megabooks, megabucks, megagood, megawork.* "That teacher is such a *megabitch.*"

PERMA- Permanent: *permagrin, permagross, permanerve, permaproblem.* "After just two beers, she had *permagrin* ."

-AGE Noun suffix which does not change the meaning of the word to which it is attached: *bookage, buckage, fundage, snowage, tunage.* "I'm desperate for *foodage.*"

-AHOLIC A person who indulges excessively in the noun to which the suffix is attached: *bookaholic, cokeaholic, foodaholic, hoopaholic.* "Sue is such a *hoopaholic* she carries a basketball in her car at all times."

-DOM The domain of: *fratdom, geekdom, jockdom.* "Walking through the computer building is a trip through *geekdom.*"

-ER One who or that which.

BUMMER Depressing experience. "Studying on Thursday nights is a *bummer.*"

DOPER Associated with smoking marijuana. "The *doper* music is loud tonight."

HOOKER Tow truck. "The *hooker* got me for parking in the state vehicles' spot."

LOOKER Attractive male or female. "There are a couple of *lookers* in my English class."

WANKER Undesirable person, thing, or situation. "Don't read that book—it's a real *wanker.*"

-FEST An abundance of: *beerfest, pizzafest, sleepfest.* "I just got paid. *Pizzafest,* everyone!"

-EY, -IE   One who or that which.

DESKIE   Desk attendant in a dormitory. "He's a *deskie* at James."

GROUPIE   Follower, idolizer. "Granville Towers is filled with basketball *groupies*."

GRUNGIE   Someone who wears old, shabby, dirty-looking clothes. "Those motorcycle freaks are *grungies*."

HOMEY   Someone from the same town or a longtime friend. "I want you to meet one of my *homies*."

Veggie

VEGGIE   Someone who *vegs out*, i.e., acts like a vegetable. "When I finish this paper, I'm just going to be a *veggie*."

-OMATIC   Emphatic suffix: *cramomatic, dunkomatic, jamomatic, jogomatic*. "I have to *cramomatic* for Dr. Joyner's English test."

-ORAMA   Emphatic suffix: *barforama, funorama, geekorama, sexorama*. "She gave us a fourteen-page take-home test — *barforama!*"

WORD ACTION:
Putting Words Together

Putting words together into a new compound word or into a unified phrase is an ancient and ongoing process in English. The three categories of words and phrases in this section show that compounding is a productive process in slang as well. In the first group, the nouns that form the second member of the compound have general, stereotypic meanings like suffixes and combine freely with a wide range of words.

For example, the element *-city* indicates merely "a presence or abundance of," not "a metropolis" and can be added to almost any kind of word. The second group illustrates less predictable combinations of two words into one, sometimes with figurative meanings, e.g., *lunchbox*, (one who is not aware of what is going on). The third type of compound is the most frequent, combining a word of any part of speech with a little invariant word like *out, up, down, on, off*.

-ACTION   Activity.
"I'm ready for some Chinese *food action*."
"Check out the *volleyball action*."

-ANIMAL   One who does something excessively.
"That *party animal* cruises Franklin Street every night."
"The *study animals* are complaining about the noise."

-CITY   A presence or abundance of.
"The day after spring break it was *tan city*."
"Even when she plays tennis, she's *jewelry city*."

-DUDE   A person. "Somebody pay the *pizza dude*." (The one who delivers pizza.)

-DWELLER Someone who frequents a particular place. "She's one of the *stand dwellers*." (She hangs around the life guard stand.) "I could hardly get into Lenoir Hall because of the *step dwellers*."

-HEAD Person. "Check out the shoes on that *tackhead*." (Male who dresses in pimp-like clothes and thinks he's cool.) "The *potheads* were in the corner mellowing out." (One who smokes marijuana, i.e., pot.)

-MACHINE An enthusiast, a devotee. "After Thanksgiving I'll be a *study-machine*." "That *sex-machine* keeps phoning Karen even though I told him she went home this weekend."

-QUEEN Female enthusiast. "Miss *Partyqueen* woke me up when she came in at 5 AM." "The *datequeen* slept through class this morning and wanted to copy my notes."

-WAD Dense, dull, foolish person. "Joe is such a *dipwad* — who invited him to the party?" "*Mikewad* here locked himself out of the room."

· ·

ALL-NIGHTER Entire night spent without sleep to study or write a paper. "After I pulled an *all-nighter* to finish the paper, the teacher gave the whole class an extension."

BAT CAVE To sleep. "Tim's been *bat caving* all afternoon because he partied all night."

BONG-BREATH — Someone who takes advantage of another. "Leave my cigarette alone, you *bong-breath*." (A *bong* is a pipe used to smoke marijuana and other herbs.)

BUTT-LOAD — Large quantity. "It just cost me a *buttload* of money to get my motorcycle fixed."

CHEESE-MAN — An out-of-style, socially inept person. Also CHEESEBAG, CHEESEFACE, CHEESEHEAD, CAPTAIN CHEDDAR, CHEESE WHIZ. "That stereo salesman was a real *cheeseman*."

Zipperhead

COOL WHIP — Something very new and appealing. "That new flick is *cool whip*."

DINGLE-BERRY — A socially inept person. "Tell that *dingleberry* I'm not here."

DOY-BURGER — Someone who is dim-witted or physically uncoordinated. "That usher-dude is such a *doyburger*."

EARTH DADDY — Older-than-college-age male who displays a 60's style mellowness, wears a beard, and attends college parties.

HOMEBOY — Someone from the same hometown, a long-time friend, or someone who shares the same values. Also HOME, HOMESLICE, HOMES, SHERLOCK (from Sherlock Holmes). "One of my *homeboys* is coming for the weekend."

HOME BISCUIT	Good friend. "Yo, *home biscuit*, let's go shoot some hoop."
HOT DOG	One who tries to impress others by dominating a situation. To show off, particularly in sports. "Coach Smith doesn't allow *hot dogging* on his team."
JACKSHIT	Nothing. "I didn't do *jackshit* on my paper this weekend."
MOUNTAIN CLIMBER	High induced by drugs. "Don't mess with this *mountain climber*."
RAGMAN/ RAGWOMAN	Person in a bad mood. "Jim is such a *ragman* that I hate to be around him."
REDNECK	Conservative, white, rural Southerner. "I'm a wreck. Some *redneck* in a pickup kept riding my bumper all the way from Pittsboro."
RICEBURNER	Japanese motorcycle.
ROAD TRIP	A spur-of-the-moment trip anywhere, usually after a party. "We took a *roadtrip* to the beach this morning to get some donuts."
SAND-BAGGED	Thrown out of one's room so that one's roommate can have an amorous encounter. "Bill's girlfriend came up for the weekend and Bob got *sandbagged* again."
ZIPPER-HEAD	A male with an out-of-style haircut, e.g., parted down the middle. "That *zipperhead* needs to catch the CLUE BUS."

. . . .

BEAM OUT	To daydream. "Oh, I'm sorry. I was *beaming out* and didn't hear what you said."
BLOW OUT	To shock, embarrass. "When she got drunk at the party, she really *blew* her date *out*."

BOMB OUT To fail, perform poorly. "He really *bombed out* by forgetting their date."

BUM OUT To cause or experience unpleasant feelings or bad reactions. "This English 2 research paper really *bums* me *out*."

BURN OUT To become mentally or physically exhausted. "Rush was fun, but I'm *burned out* from it."

CHECK OUT To look at, observe. "Let's go *check out* the fox factor at the mixer."

CHILL OUT To relax, calm down. "Hey, *chill out*, man, I was only kidding." Also CHILL, TAKE A CHILL PILL.

CRANK OUT To produce large amounts of work, energy, volume. "The band at the all-campus could really *crank out* the jams."

GEEK OUT To study hard.

GOOB OUT To cause repulsion or disgust. "Joe got sick in the car — he really *goobed* me *out*."

Jell Out

JELL OUT To relax by doing nothing, i.e., by acting like jello. "Bob just *jelled out* all weekend." Also VEG OUT.

LAY OUT To sunbathe. "Check the babes *laying out* behind the dorm."

LUDE OUT To become unable to function or physically incapacitated. (Probably derived from the drug name *Quaalude*.) "He was so *luded out* he couldn't get the key in his door."

PHASE OUT To become unaware, as if asleep. "I *phased out* during that lecture about footnotes this morning."

PLASTIC OUT To assume temporarily an artificial behavior or personality. "Beth began to *plastic out* when she realized it was Dave's mother on the phone."

RAG OUT To become tired. "I *ragged out* when I ran those four miles on just two hours of sleep."

RAUNCH OUT To offend by making sexual remarks or using offensive language. "Peter thinks he's cool, but he just *raunches* me *out*."

ROCK OUT To play music loudly. "My roommate loves to *rock out* when she does her homework."

SMELL OUT To interview. "We're going to *smell out* the rush chairman today."

SNORT OUT To overeat. "The four of us ordered pizza and really *snorted out*."

SPAZ OUT To lose mental control. "I *spazzed out* during the Chem final."

SCHIZ OUT To lose emotional control, to act crazed. "Lisa started *schizzing out* about three hours before the exam."

SUE OUT To dress and look like a stereotypic sorority member. "I think I'll *sue out* today and wear my add-a-beads."

TANG OUT To abandon, put an end to. "I'm going to *tang* *out* on the books and catch some z's."

TRIP OUT   To strike as funny, crazy, or extraordinary. "That film last night *tripped* me *out*."

WEIRD OUT   To feel confused and at a loss because of someone's or something's strangeness. "I was *weirded out* when she said she was looking forward to a painful death."

WIG OUT   To become astonished. "When I saw the price of my textbooks I *wigged out*."

Wig Out

WIMP OUT   To let someone down; to fail to live up to a commitment. "You promised not to tell anyone. Now don't *wimp out* on us."

BAMAED UP   Very ugly. "Her boyfriend is one *bamaed up* dude."

BEAM UP   To die. "The doctors tried to save him, but he just *beamed up*."

BURN UP   To put in a complete effort or do fast. "I was so hungry I *burned up* Wendy's taco bar."

CAFF UP   To become hyperactive because of too much caffeine. "During my English exam I was so *caffed up* I could hardly sit still."

CASH UP   To solve, think through, analyze. "Louie asked me to *cash up* the Chem problems for him."

EAT UP   Temporarily physically unattractive. "Laura pulled an ALL-NIGHTER and looked *eat up* in her 9 o'clock class."

JACK UP   To use force. "You do that again, and I'll *jack* you *up*."

LIGHTEN UP   To stop annoying or bothering. "Would you *lighten up* about my smoking?"

MOMMY UP   To love, hug, comfort. "His girlfriend *mommied* him *up* when he stepped off the plane."

PUMP UP   Inspire, energize, stimulate. "Phil Ford could always *pump up* the team."

SCREW UP   To bungle, to make a mistake; "They really *screwed up* student seating in the Dean Dome."

BITE ON   To copy someone else, particularly in clothing. "Susan is *biting on* my earrings."

BUST ON   To criticize, poke fun at. "Would you quit *busting on* my date?"

CRACK ON   To embarrass or humiliate. "Bill kept *cracking on* Joan about locking the keys in the car." To make romantic overtures. "That geek kept *cracking on* Jane, so we had to leave."

DISS ON   To criticize, belittle. "I'm tired of John *dissing on* her all the time."

HARSH ON   To criticize, belittle, act ungraciously. "Don't *harsh on* me for making noise — it's almost noon."

LATCH ON   To understand. "If I can't *latch on* to physics soon, I'm in big trouble."

LIVE ON   To take pleasure from the embarrassment of another. "When I fell off my bike in the middle

26

of campus, my roommate *lived on* it all day."

RAG ON   To reprimand, insult. "Our professor *ragged on* us for reading the DTH in class." Also RAIL ON.

RIFF ON   To take advantage of another. "Hey, don't *riff on* me, man, just because I'm sick."

TURN ON   To use some sort of drugs. "My roommate *turns on* every day before grammar class." To cause interest or excitement. "The Red Clay Ramblers can *turn* this local audience *on*."

BLOW OFF   To forget, ignore, absent oneself. "I haven't read the novel we're talking about, so I'm going to *blow off* English class."

DINK OFF   To make angry. "It *dinks* me *off* when you yell at me."

GET OFF   To become excited, have fun. "Coye was *getting off* at Purdy's last night."

GO OFF ON   To show anger at. "Pat *went off on* John for breaking the exercise bike."

Bust On

SLANGUAGE:
Putting Pieces of Words Together

Sometimes new words are made by putting pieces of words together and combining the meanings of the original words. Examples from everyday language are **brunch**, from **breakfast** and **lunch**, and names created for products, like **applecran** juice and the **croissandwich**.

BUEL   Food; to eat voraciously. From **body** + **fuel**. "Let's go **buel** on some Hector's."

DRONED   Unaware because of alcohol or drugs. From **drink** + **stoned**. "He was so **droned** he thought his date was his mother."

Homechop

HOMECHOP An endearing term for a close friend, usually of the opposite sex. From **homeboy/homegirl** + **lambchop**. "Yo, Michelle. What's up, **homechop**?"

SPADET   A student preoccupied with studies. From **space** + **cadet**. "My roommate's off booking with the other **spadets** in the class."

SPORK Eating implement. From *spoon + fork*. "I wonder why someone invented these stupid plastic *sporks*."

SWEAVE To have difficulty walking straight. From *swerve + weave*. "Scot was *sweaving* after pounding a six-pack."

VOMATOSE Disgusting. From *vomit + comatose*. "Sean downed so many mixed drinks he was *vomatose* the whole weekend."

TO THE MIN:
Shortening Words and Phrases

By the process of shortening, sounds are eliminated from words without a loss of meaning. Many ordinary English words have been formed in this way: *fan* from *fanatic*, *flu* from *influenza*, and *phone* from *telephone*. Most of the time, the meaning of the shortened form is the same as that of the longer word from which it was derived.

BOD From *body*.

BRARY From *library*.

BRO, BROTH From *brother*.

CATCH A VID To watch music videos on MTV. "Let's go to the lounge and *catch a vid*." From *catch a music video*.

CAZH Relaxing, conducive to good times. "I heard that was a *cazh* birthday party." From *casual*.

COKE From *cocaine*.

FEEB Dull-witted or absent-minded person. From *feeble*.

FILE   To show off; to dress up. "Did you see what Nicholas has on? Man, he's *filing*." From *profile*.

FRIZ   From *frisbee*.

GIG   From *gigolo*.

HYPER   From *hyperactive*.

IG   From *ignore*.

MESC   From *mescaline*.

NARK   From *narcotics agent*.

OBNO   From *obnoxious*.

PREESH   Thanks. "*Preesh* for telling my mom I was at the library." From *appreciate*.

PRESH   Favorable, enjoyable. "That late night was *presh*." From *precious*. Also rhymes with *fresh*.

RAD   Excellent. From *radical*.

RENT, RENTAL UNIT   From *parental unit*, mock sociological jargon popularized by *Saturday Night Live*.

RENTS   From *parents*.

SPAZ   A clumsy person, usually said jokingly. From *spastic*.

TIVES   From *relatives*.

TO THE MAX   From *to the maximum*.

VIBES   Inaudible signals that people and places emit. From *vibrations*.

WELK   From *you're welcome*.

N. B. D.:
Words from Letters

In an extreme form of shortening called acronymy, words are made from the initial letters of the words in a phrase. For example, the United States of America is named by the letters U.S.A.; however, in the acronym SCUBA, from *self-contained underwater breathing apparatus,* the letters are pronounced together as a word. Both ways of forming words from letters also occur in slang.

B. K. LOUNGE From *Burger King.*

B. L. From *Big Library.*

D. H. C. From *deep heavy conversation.*

G. H. From the soap opera *General Hospital.*

G. Q. Fashionably and tastefully dressed. "Dean Floyd always looks so *G. Q.*" From *Gentlemen's Quarterly.*

H. D. Male who mooches off a female. From the military designation *husband dependent.*

J. Marijuana cigarette. From *joint.*

K. O. Die. From *kick off.*

M. D. G. Strong physical attraction, not dependent on feelings of love or friendship. "Libby and Billy have an M. D. G." From *mutual desire to grope.*

M. L. A.

M. L. A. Passionate kissing. From *massive lip action.*

M. R. A. Unsociable behavior. From *major reeb action*.

N. B. D. From *no big deal*.

N. C. A boorish person. From *no class*.

N. C. A. A. From *no class at all*. Pronounced "n.c. double a."

N. F. From *no fun*.

N. T. S. Good-looking male. From *name tag shaker*. "That Jack is one power *N.T.S.*"

O. D. From *overdose*.

O. O. C. Drunk, high on drugs, or acting crazy. From *out of control*.

O. T. L. Inattentive, unaware. From *out to lunch*.

O. T. R. Snappish, in a bad mood. Originally applied to females but now can apply to either sex. "I think Bill's *O. T. R.* today because of problems at home." From *on the rag*.

P. D. K. Someone who is out of date or out of touch. From *polyester double knit*.

P. F. MATERIAL Good-looking male. From *pledge formal material*.

P. Q. Someone who is out of date. From *polyester queen*.

R. & I. Extremely exciting and enjoyable. From *radical and intense*.

S. A. B. From *social airhead bitch*.

TAN Aggressively masculine. From *tough as nails*.

T. S. H. From *that shit happens*.

V. P. L. From *visible panty lines*, from a Woody Allen film.

BUDWIPER:
Playing with Sounds

In the creative use of language, speakers often play with sounds, using onomatopoeia or imitation, alliteration, rhyme, dialect pronunciations, and puns — devices commonly associated with poetry. Slang, too, plays with sound in these ways, and poets like Walt Whitman and Carl Sandburg have pointed out the similarity between the linguistic creativity of slang and poetry.

Onomatopoeia

BARF   Vomit, sound of regurgitation.

JING   Money. From *jingle*.

RALPH   Vomit. Sound of regurgitation.

SSSSSS—   A hissing sound to indicate that someone is acting like an *airhead*.

YUCK   Imitation of gagging over something disgusting.

Alliteration

BAD BONGOS Situation in which things do not go well. "That English test was *bad bongos*."

BIBLE BEATER An evangelizing fundamentalist Christian. "That same *Bible beater* was in The Pit again today."

BLIMP BOAT Obese person.

GROUP GROPES Encounter groups.

ROMPER ROOM A place to get rowdy and wild. Allusion to a children's television program of the 1950's.

Rhyme

BALLS TO THE WALLS A tense, if not frantic, time or situation which requires the ability to fight back. "From now until the end of the month, it's *balls to the walls*."

Group Gropes

BEAT THE FEET To hurry up.

COME IN, BERLIN A request to someone who isn't paying attention.

FAKE AND BAKE To get a tan in a tanning booth.

GODSQUAD People who preach on campus.

GROOMED TO ZOOM Very well dressed.

HELL DWELL	To have a good time drinking and partying at local pubs.
JAP SCRAP	Motorcycle; appliance made in Japan.
LATER, TATER	Goodby.
POP TOPS	To drink beer.
SIGHT DELIGHT	Good-looking male.
SLOP SHOP	Any campus snack bar.
STYLIN' AND PROFILIN'	Very well dressed and groomed.
TAKE A CHILL PILL	Calm down, relax.
TIGHTY-WHITIES	Men's briefs.

Phonetic Alterations and Plans

BRARY DOG	One who studies in the library. Allusion to *prairie dog*.
BRRRR RABBIT	An expression used when it's very cold. Allusion to Br'er Rabbit.
BUD-WIPER	A beer. Alteration of brand name *Budweiser*.
EGG-A-MUFFIN	A response indicating agreement with what has been said. X: "There's an awesome party at the Union — wanna go?" Y: "*Egg-a-muffin!*" Alteration of *Egg McMuffin* from McDonald's.

OZONE RANGER	Someone who is out of touch with reality. Alteration of *The Lone Ranger*, a radio and television serial.
THE PLOT SICKENS	Things are getting worse. Alteration of the cliche *the plot thickens*.
SCREWS ME	Alteration of *excuse me*.

Mock Dialect Pronunciations

RAW'S	*Roy's*, from Roy Roger's Restaurant.
WALLER	To engage in sexual activity. From *wallow*.
WROUGHT IRON	Expression of approval or enthusiasm. From *right on!*

Ozone Ranger

MERCY BUTTERCUPS:
Borrowing from Foreign Languages

Over the centuries, the main way in which the vocabulary of English has grown has been by borrowing words and pieces of words from foreign languages. Ordinary words like *are*, *take* and *wine* as well as more erudite words like *bibliophile*, *detente*, and *epistemology* are all the result of borrowing. In this respect, slang differs from language in general, for slang rarely acquires new words by borrowing, except in greetings and in playful mispronunciations of foreign expressions.

| **CIAO** | Goodby. From Italian. |
| **ESCARGO** | Male walking arm-in-arm with his date. Used humorously. Allusion to French *escargot* (snail) and English *his cargo*. |

FAUX	To make a mistake. "I really *fauxed* that time." From French *faux pas*.
GRACI	Thanks. From Italian *graci*.
GUIDO	Male attempting to be macho. From the Italian proper name *Guido*. "That fraternity is full of *guidos*."
LEGUME	Person who is tired, out of energy, acting like a vegetable. From French *legume* (vegetable).
LUEGO	Goodby. From Spanish.
MONGE OUT	To overeat. From French *manger* (to eat).
MERCY BUTTER-CUPS	Thank you. From French *merci beaucoup*.
MY FEET ARE STAYIN'	Goodby. From German *auf wiedersehen*.
OSMOSIS AMOEBAS	Goodby. From Spanish *adios amigos*.
PAUL REVERE	Goodby. From French *au revoir*.
SARAJEVO	Goodby. From *Sarajevo*, Yugoslavia, site of the 1984 winter Olympics. Phonetic alteration of *sayonara*.
SEAFOOD PLATE	Please. From French *S'il vous plait*.
SLACK-MEISTER	Habitual procrastinator. Compound of *slack* and German *meister* (master).

Seafood Plate

37

RAPPING:
Borrowing from Black English

Although college slang seldom borrows from foreign languages, it does borrow readily from the variety of American English spoken by many Blacks and sometimes called Black English. American English in general has borrowed usages from Blacks, particularly from jazz musicians and entertainers. Probably the best known examples are the use of *bad* to mean "good" and other ironic interpretations of words like *mean* and *wicked*. College slang likewise finds Black English a rich source for new words and expressions.

BAD   Good. "Tanya had a *bad* ride."

BE ILLIN'   Confused, upset, irritated, angry. "Louie be illin' about that exam grade."

BLOOD   Fellow Black; friend. "Yo, Blood."

BLOW   To sing well. "Have you heard Maggie sing? She can really *blow*."

BOSS   Superior, excellent. "That red Corvette is *boss*."

CLEAN   Well dressed. "Marilyn sure did come to class *clean* today."

DIG   Understand. "I *dig* where you're coming from."

FRONT   Pretend to be something one is not. "Stop *fronting*. You know you like her."

HAWK   Wind. "The *hawk* ain't JIVING." (It's windy.)

JAM   To play or listen to music; to dance; to have a good time; to perform well. "I was really *jammin'* on that test today."

JIVE   To give someone misinformation or false impressions. "Man, don't you *jive* me."

THE JOINT The best, the most popular. "Everybody was at Marilyn's when Roger was in town — it was *the joint*."

JUKE Dance. "They really *juke* at the Bacchae on Thursdays."

Mainsqueeze

MAIN-SQUEEZE Favorite girlfriend or boyfriend. "Chuck was JAMMIN' with his *mainsqueeze*."

RAP To talk seriously. "The guys in the suite *rapped* for hours last night and planned all our lives."

SLAVE A job. "I guess I'll check out this *slave* for the summer."

STONE FOX Extremely beautiful woman. "Phil's got him one *stone fox* tonight."

WHAT IT IS? Greeting.

PERPETRATING:
Ordinary Words with Different Meanings

For the most part, slang items are words already in the language which take on a different meaning in slang. Such change in meaning is accomplished by a variety of processes operative in the language in general, including shifts in meaning, allusion, irony, and figurative use.

Shifts

For some words, shifts in meaning and the connection among multiple meanings of the same word are easy to understand. Thus the word *sight* refers both to "the sense of seeing" and to "that which is seen." Slang customarily uses words from the general vocabulary with shifted meanings. For some words connections are easy to guess. The slang meaning of *budget*, for example, as "inferior" can be plausibly explained as a series of shifts. Other changes in meaning are not so easy to imagine, for example *art* meaning "goodby."

ARBITRARY Insignificant. "He's just *arbitrary* in my life."

ART Finished, departed; goodby. "Outta here — you're *art*." Perhaps fashioned on *you're history* or *you're archives*.

BOGUS Peculiar, awkward, stupid; unfair. "She had on the most *bogus* dress you've ever seen." "That test was *bogus*."

BUDGET Inadequate, not up to standard. "They didn't print my favorite comic in the paper today — *budget!*"

CRUCIAL Superior, exciting. "The annual Burnout is a *crucial* party."

DERELICT A dull-witted person. "Don't go out with Mike — he's such a *derelict*."

DISCIPLINE Dope, marijuana. "I need some *discipline* badly."

EASY Flexible, not difficult to please. "Would you like to go today or tomorrow? I'm *easy*."

HEALTHY Very pretty. "Check her out, man, she's *healthy*."

HEINOUS Unpleasant, negative, ugly. "That food was *heinous*."

JUSTICE Out of the ordinary, cool. "Those babes are *justice*."

LAME Unfortunate, undesirable, "It's so *lame* that I have two tests tomorrow and can't go to Purdy's with you."

MAIN-STREAM	Mediocre; preoccupied with respectability and materialistic values. "It's a *mainstream* movie — don't waste your time."
PEG	To speak unfavorably about. "It's good he wasn't at the party because he was really *pegged*."
PERPE-TRATE	To pretend. "That's not an engagement ring — she's just *perpetrating*."
RADICAL	Unexpectedly wild. "We all got pretty *radical* at the pledge formal."
RANDOM	Undesirable. "This is one *random* pen I'm writing with."
SCARY	Unappealing, in bad taste. "Lillian had on this *scary* polka-dot hairbow today."
SOLID	A favor. "Do me a *solid*, will you?"
TALK	To date. "Louie and Tanya are *talking*."
TIGHT	Good-looking, attractive. "Renee's wig is *tight*."

QUIZ: The Familiar Made Strange

Match letters on right to numbers on left.

1.	**PERPETRATE**	A.	**Mediocre**
2.	**BUDGET**	B.	**Unfortunate, undesirable**
3.	**TIGHT**	C.	**Unexpectedly wild**
4.	**LATCH ON**	D.	**A favor**
5.	**JUSTICE**	E.	**To pretend**
6.	**A SOLID**	F.	**Understand**
7.	**MAINSTREAM**	G.	**Inadequate, shoddy**
8.	**TALK**	H.	**Out of the ordinary; cool**

9. LAME	I. To date
10. RADICAL	J. Good-looking; attractive

Allusion

Often the meaning of a slang expression draws on knowledge of segments of the culture important to the speakers. For college students, the sources of allusion tend to be films, television, and music. Sometimes a slang expression is taken directly from a source, as *bodacious ta-tas* (breasts) from the film *An Officer and a Gentleman*. In other instances, the allusion is more complicated, as in *Land's End*, an all-purpose exclamation that draws on the colloquialism *land's sake* and the name of a popular and fashionable mail order company.

BARBIE AND KEN An impeccably groomed and attired, but unimaginative and conventional, couple. From the *Barbie* and *Ken* dolls.

BEAM ME UP, SCOTTY A wish to be elsewhere. From *Star Trek*.

BEAV AND WALLY Names that males call each other in jest. From the little brother/big brother relationship on the television series *Leave It to Beaver*.

BODACIOUS TA-TAS Shapely breasts. From the film *An Officer and a Gentleman*.

Beam Me Up, Scotty

BOGART   To take an unfair share, particularly of a marijuana cigarette; to borrow or steal. From the tough guy characters played by Humphrey Bogart, popularized in a song by Little Feat, "Don't *Bogart* that JOINT, Man."

BRING IT ALL BACK HOME   To go out and have a good time. From Bob Dylan's "Bringing It All Back Home."

BRUCE   A male who thinks he's cool but really isn't. "All right, *Bruce*, cut out the slick routine." From the actor Bruce Willis (David Addison on the television series *Moonlighting*.)

BULL-GOOSE LOONY   Out of control, usually in a more amusing than destructive fashion. "You done run *bull-goose loony*, boy — don't you point that fire extinguisher at me." From Ken Kesey's *One Flew Over the Cuckoo's Nest*.

COULD IT BE — SATAN?   Humorous response to something naughty. "And who is responsible for that? *Could it be — Satan?*" From the Church Lady on *Saturday Night Live*.

DUNLOP SYNDROME   Fat ("spare tire") around the waist. "Looks like Tom has contracted *Dunlop Syndrome*." From *Dunlop* brand of tire.

FROM CHICAGO   An AIRHEAD; out of touch with what's going on. "Nobody noticed the sink overflowing? All of you must be *from Chicago*." Allusion to Chicago, the Windy City.

G-FORCE   Expression of agreement.
X: "Let's go to Franklin St."
Y: "G-Force!" From the Japanese comic strip *G-Force*."

GH ATTACK   Strong desire to shirk all responsibilities in order to watch *General Hospital*, an afternoon soap opera.

GOGGLE-BOX   Eager NERD. "Those do-goody *goggleboxes* in Student Government didn't help me at all." From the film *Repo Man*.

Gogglebox

GUMBEY-HEAD   Person who does something stupid. Usually said in jest. From a green doll later portrayed by Eddie Murphy on *Saturday Night Live*.

IN THE TWILIGHT ZONE   Confused. "After the test I was in *the twilight zone*." Allusion to the television series *The Twilight Zone*.

JETSON   A SPACE CADET, someone who is out of touch with what is going on. From the character *George Jetson* on a television cartoon series set in space.

THE KIDS The television soap opera *All My Children*.

KNOW WHAT I MEAN, VERN? Expression asking for agreement. From a popular series of television commercials.

LAND'S END All purpose exclamation. "*Land's End!* The phone is ringing again." From the name of a popular and fashionable mail order company.

LIM-BURGER A girl no one else will date. From the song "Dance This Mess Around" by the B-52's.

NIP IT Stop. "Lawrence Welk? *Nip it* and play some Rick Jones." From Barney Fife's *nip it in the bud* with reference to jaywalking in Mayberry, from *The Andy Griffith Show*.

OK, SPOCK An indication that the addressee is acting too erudite or putting on airs. From the character Mr. Spock on *Star Trek*.

OTIS Drunk. From *Otis*, the town drunk of Mayberry, on *The Andy Griffith Show*.

PSYCH! Acknowledgement of a successful joke or trick. "Want my candy bar? *Psych!*" From an Eddie Murphy comedy routine.

REAL MAN A macho man, who doesn't eat such wimpy foods as quiche. From the title of the book *Real Men Don't Eat Quiche*.

SURE, I KNEW YOU COULD An expression of doubt, used sarcastically. In imitation of Mr. Rogers on the children's television program.

USE UP ALL MY LETTERS To demonstrate intellectual superiority. "When I brought up Legare's cis-Alpine discipline in class, I really *used up all my letters*." Allusion to the game *Scrabble*.

WILMA   Stupid female. "This *Wilma* in front of me stood all during the concert." From the cartoon character on *The Flintstones*.

QUIZ: Allusions

Match letters on right to numbers on left.

1. BODACIOUS TA-TAS
2. GH ATTACK
3. LIMBURGER
4. BRUCE
5. BULL-GOOSE LOONY
6. OTIS
7. FROM CHICAGO
8. BARBIE AND KEN
9. BEAM ME UP, SCOTTY
10. JETSON

A. A wish to be elsewhere
B. Out of control
C. Drunk
D. An airhead
E. Conventional people
F. Someone out of touch with reality
G. A female no one else will date
H. A male who thinks he's cool but is not
I. Shapely female breasts
J. Strong desire to skip class and watch *General Hospital*

Answers: 1 I; 2 J; 3 G; 4 H; 5 B; 6 C; 7 D; 8 E; 9 A; 10 F

Irony

One kind of irony is the use of words to convey the contrary or opposite of their ordinary meaning. In the language as a whole, negative irony is often signalled by a sarcastic tone of voice.

BAD	Very good. "Phil Ford was such a *bad* ball handler."
BOGUS	Positive, outstanding. "Taking a ROADTRIP to the beach was such a *bogus* idea." Negative, unpleasant. "That test was *bogus*."
BOYSCOUT	A punk or drug user.
EARTH PEOPLE	People who are not in touch with reality, who still wear Earth Shoes.
GROOVER	Someone who is behind the times in fashions, who still says *groovy*.
HURT ME	An expression used by males to evaluate the looks of females. Can be either positive or negative depending on the intonation.
I'M SHAKING	Expression of pseudo-fear. X: "Lighten up or I'll cram this beer down your throat." Y: "*I'm shaking*."
KILLER	Very bad or very good. "That was a *killer* test!" or "That's a *killer* beer!"
LIFER	Someone arrested for a minor infraction or given a traffic ticket. "You got busted for public drunkenness? You *lifer*."
MEAN	Cool, fashionable. "Michael Jordan is one *mean* dude on the cover of *GQ*."
SPECIAL	Unpleasant, awkward. "I ran into my ex-boyfriend with my best friend — it was real *special*."

Figurative Language

Figurative language designates a meaning by words previously used to refer to something else. For example, speakers are using figurative language when they ***put an***

idea on the back burner, using vocabulary from the domain of cooking to describe a mental activity.

Metaphors and metonyms are kinds of figurative language found in all levels of discourse, from formal lectures to the speech of a two-year-old. Metaphors call one thing by the name of another: a ***mouse*** on a computer is not "a rodent" but "a pointing device." Metonyms designate one thing by the name of something associated with it: when ***the White House*** issues a statement, it is "the official inhabitant of the White House" who is speaking, not the house itself.

Images, mental conceptions held in common by members of a group and indicative of a basic attitude, also guide the selection of words. In English, for example, overindulgence in alcohol is expressed in images of destruction: ***annihilated, bombed, ripped, stoned***. College slang abounds in all of these kinds of figurative language.

A & P Suitcase

Metaphors

A & P SUITCASE   Grocery bag used for packing clothes for a trip.

AX   Guitar.

BANANA   Person who acts idiotic or foolish. Also JUST OFF THE BANANA BOAT.

BANANA FACTORY   Hectic, horrible, futile situation or event.

BUBBLE-GUM   Light, unimaginative, frivolous. "Turn off that *bubblegum* music."

BUBBLE-GUM MAN   Policeman.

BUBBLE-GUM MACHINE   Police car.

BUTTER COOKIES   An off-brand of athletic shoes.

CHEESE   Marijuana.

DAGGER   Pocket-sized Bible; New Testament. A smaller version of a SWORD.

DEAD SOLDIER   Empty beer can.

DO 12 OZ. CURLS   Drink beer. Allusion to lifting hand weights.

HORN   Telephone.

LIVE EYE   Television camera.

MAD DOG   Cheap wine. Originally derived from *Mogen David*.

POPSICLE STAND   Any place. "Let's blow this *popsicle stand*." Also TACO STAND.

ROACH   The butt of a marijuana cigarette.

SCAB   Person who lives off of his or her friends.

SKEETER Someone with lots of energy who flits around and tends to be bothersome. From *mosquito*.

SNOW Cocaine.

SOFA SPUD Person who lounges around, usually in front of the television, doing nothing but eating and drinking. Also SOFA YAM. From COUCH POTATO.

SQUASH BLOSSOM Pretty female.

STEM Someone who is exhausted, burned out.

SWORD A Bible. Allusion to Hebrews 4:12, "For the word of God is quick and powerful, and sharper than any two-edged sword."

TELE- PHONE Toilet.

YELLOW JACKET Nembutol, a kind of drug.

Metonyms

BLACK AND WHITE Police car.

BOX Large, box-shaped, portable radio/ cassette player.

BREW Beer.

CANCER STICK Cigarette.

Skeeter

COOL
DOPE   A soft drink. In the South, many older people call carbonated cola beverages *dopes*.

COOL ONE Beer.

DENTIST Slow, boring, uninteresting music.
OFFICE
MUSIC

DROPPED Going steady, i.e., wearing someone's fraternity lavaliere.

Fern

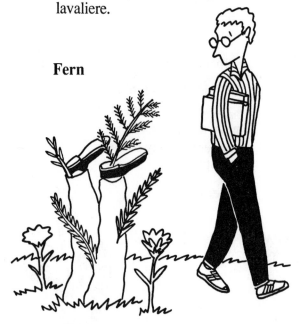

FERN   A person concerned with environmental issues; the opposite of a Yuppie.

FLICK   Film.

GRANOLA A person committed to values of the 60's, i.e., someone who eats health foods like granola; out of date.

KICKS   Gym shoes.

PUMP   Lift weights.
IRON

RIDE	Car.
SHADES	Sunglasses.
SOAP OPERA SPREAD	Weight gain from inactivity.
STORY	A television soap opera.
THREADS	Clothes.
TUBE	Television.
THE WEED	Marijuana.
WHEELS	Car.
Z-OUT	To go to sleep.

Images

THE CAMPUS ZOO:
Dogs and Other Animals

ZOO	To fail or to get the worse possible grade on a test.
THE ZOO	The undergraduate library.
ZOOED	Drunk.
ANIMAL	One who does something excessively: *party animal, study animal.*

Dogs

DOG Someone or something unattractive or unappealing. "Avocado bubblegum is a *dog*." Make the grade D or do poorly. "I *dogged* on the Chem exam." Perform well, defeat an adversary. "Ted said he didn't study but ended up *dogging* the test and blew the curve." "I *dogged* him at racquetball though."

DOG ON	Verbally abuse. "My roommate was dogging on me for using up her shampoo."
DOG IT	For a female to act sexually loose or promiscuous.
THAT DOG'LL HUNT	Expression of approval or agreement. X: "Let's order out for pizza." Y: "*That dog'll hunt.*"
LIKE A BIG DOG	With intensity: "I was running *like a big dog* to catch my bus."
THE BIG DOGMAS	The intramural sports team representing the Catholic student center.
BITCH	To complain; an unpleasant female or situation.
BITCHIN'	Mean spirited. "What a *bitchin'* exam." Attractive. "What a *bitchin'* dress."
BOWSER	Someone with an ugly face.
BRARY DOG	Someone who studies in the library. Allusion to *prairie dog*.
BREW DOG	Beer.
BREW-DOGGER	Someone who drinks too much.
CHILLY DOG	Beer.
CORNDOG	Someone who is socially inept or who acts weird.
DOG CUSS	To berate.
HOOCH DOG	A marijuana cigarette. Also JIMMY DOG, JAMES EARL DOG.
HOUND	A sexually loose or promiscuous male.
MAD DOG	Cheap wine.

Brary Dog

MUD PUPPY — Very ugly female.

PIG DOG — Someone who eats a lot.

PUPPY — Someone who falls behind the rest of the crowd.

RUN WITH THE BIG DOGS — To do anything that anyone else does.

SHROOM-DOG — Someone who uses hallucinogens.

SLOUNGE PUPPY — Lazy person.

TURD POODLE — Disagreeable person.

WIMP DOG — Male with little personality.

Porcine Creature

BOO-HOG Obese female.

HOG Sexually attractive male; a Harley-Davidson motorcycle.

OINKER Person who is overweight. Also PORKER.

PIG OUT, PORK OUT Eat large quantities of food.

Other Animals

ALLIGATOR Someone who identifies with fraternity and sorority life. From the alligator symbol on Izod clothing, a characteristic of preppie fashion.

APE WILD Uninhibited, usually with the aid of alcohol.

BARRACUDA Hateful, spiteful female.

BAT A cranky female, usually a teacher or mother.

BAT CAVE To sleep.

Alligator

Hog

BUG OUT	To act frantic or crazy.
CAT	Acceptable to the "in" group.
CHICK	Female.
COYOTE DATE	Woman who is so ugly that when you wake up the next morning and she's asleep on your arm, you'd rather chew your arm off than wake her up: "I've seen ugly — but that's a coyote date."
DUCK	A male of college age.
FISH	A weak or unlikable male.
FOX	Goodlooking female or, sometimes, male.
GATOR	To do a dance on the floor while wallowing in beer.
HAWK	To participate in an athletic activity for fun: "Let's go to the gym and *hawk* some ball."

LIKE A MOOSE	In a big way.
LIKE UGLY ON A MONKEY	Instinctively, automatically.
LOUNGE LIZARD	Someone who lies around doing nothing more energetic than watching television.
PLASTIC COW	Non-dairy creamer.
RAT	Resident of substandard housing, particularly a fraternity house. Also FRAT RAT.
REPTILE	Person who is somewhat bohemian and occasionally rude and obtuse.

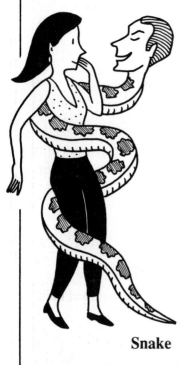

ROACH	Butt of a marijuana cigarette.
SLUG	Lazy person.
SNAKE	Flirt with someone else's date; have sex.
SQUID	Loser.
SQUIRRELY	Hyperactive, slightly crazy.
STONE FOX	Extremely beautiful female.
TURKEY	An all-around loser.
WHALE ON	Perform extremely well, defeat.
WILD BOAR	Person who indulges excessively in the pursuit of amusement. Also PARTY ANIMAL.

Snake

Frat Rat

QUIZ: Irony and Metaphor

Match letters on right to numbers on left.

1.	MEAN	A.	Toilet
2.	SKEETER	B.	Hyperactive acquaintance; pest
3.	DAGGER	C.	Awkward; unpleasant
4.	TELEPHONE	D.	Pocketsized Bible
5.	LIFER	E.	Police car
6.	SPECIAL	F.	Cool, fashionable
7.	DEAD SOLDIERS	G.	Marijuana
8.	CHEESE	H.	Guitar
9.	BUBBLEGUM MACHINE	I.	Beer cans
10.	AX	J.	Someone arrested for a minor offense

Answers: 1 F; 2 B; 3 D; 4 A; 5 J; 6 C; 7 I; 8 G; 9 E; 10 H

IN THE OZONE:
Images of Air and Space

AIR To jump high in the air as a prelude to slam-dunking a basketball. Also SKY. "Jordan is *airing* like a crazed weasel."

AIRBRAIN, AIRHEAD Person who appears dumb, has little common sense, or is unaware of what is going on. Also HELIUM HEAD.

COSMIC Extraordinary, unique, excellent.

EARTH TO- A signal that the addressee is not communicating, i.e., is *spaced out*.

FLOAT To be distant, off in thought.

IN ORBIT Out of touch with what is going on. Also IN THE OZONE, LOST IN THE OZONE, ON ANOTHER PLANE, ON ANOTHER PLANET, ON A SPACE TRIP.

SERGEANT SPACE One whose mind is ranging somewhere in space. Also OZONE RANGER.

SPACE, SPACE OUT To appear unaware of what is going on.

SPACE CADET Someone who acts spaced out. Also SPACE CASE, SPACE COOKIE, SPADET, SPACE QUEEN, SUZY SPACE SHIP.

SPACEY   Unaware.

SUZIE   An inattentive, absent-minded female.
SPACESHIP

UFO   Someone not in touch with reality; a party
crasher. From ***Unidentified Flying Object.***

ZONE,   To appear distracted, preoccupied.
ZONE OUT

Suzie Spaceship

College Slang 101

III. MEANINGS OF COLLEGE SLANG:
A Focus on Social Dimensions

Seldom do slang items contribute meanings not conveyed by words already in the language. Rather, slang tends to provide alternative words and phrases — often fresh and catchy — in a limited number of subject areas important to the slang-producing group. Furthermore, slang users are rarely satisfied with one or two variants but are constantly replenishing the store of words to capture the same limited range of meanings. The result is a large number of synonyms or near-synonyms.

The categories of meaning in this chapter show the activities that inspire slang among college students. The pursuit of knowledge figures only slightly in the special vocabulary of college students. The subjects that serve as an impetus for the proliferation of slang on college campuses instead focus on the social dimensions of the educational experience: having a good time, appearing nonchalant and fashionable, eating, drinking, seeking romance and sex, and the like. The social nature of slang also accounts for the negative spirit of many of these words; the negativity is needed to show who and what is unacceptable to the group.

TOXIC WASTE DUMP: Drugs

BLOW   Cocaine. Also BERNICE, COKE, CORINNE, CRANK, GOLD DUST, FLAKE, NOSE CANDY, PONY, SNOW, SPANISH FLY, STARDUST, SUPERFLY.

CONTACT Effect of inhaling marijuana smoke without actually smoking a joint. "I got a *contact* just walking into the bathroom."

DOOBIOUS Experiencing the effects of smoking marijuana.

ENGLISH CHANNEL EYES Blood-shot or swollen eyes caused by exposure to marijuana smoke. "I still have *English Channel eyes* from the party last night."

GRASS Marijuana. Also BONE, DOOBAGE, DOOBIE, GANGA, HERB, HOOCH, HOOCHDOG, JAMES EARL DOG, JIMMY DOG, KILLER WEED, ORGANIC STUFF, POT, SPLEEF, THE WEED.

JOINT A marijuana cigarette. Also J, J-BO, NUMBER, REEFER.

SHOTGUN Procedure in which one person puts the lighted end of a joint in his or her mouth and exhales, sending a stream of smoke which is inhaled by a second person. "That *shotgun* took my head off."

STONED High, experiencing the effects, pleasant or unpleasant, of taking drugs. Also BAKED, BLASTED, CRISPY, ETHEREAL, JACKED, OUT OF IT, RIPPED, SPACED, STRUNG OUT, ZOOTIED.

TOXIC WASTE DUMP Someone who frequently uses recreational drugs. "That *toxic waste dump* was selling stolen text books to get money."

TURN ON To smoke marijuana or to take drugs. Also FLIP OUT, FREAK OUT, GET SMALL, GET THERE, TRANSCEND, TRIP, X-OUT, ZOOM.

QUAFFING: Drinking

The single meaning that accounts for the greatest number of synonyms in the informal vocabulary of English is over-indulgence in alcohol. Synonyms for **drunk** in English cannot be counted, as new ones crop up daily and old ones tend to stay in the language for years, enjoying momentary bursts of popularity from time to time.

Here is a selection of just sixty synonyms for **drunk** in use on the Carolina campus 1972-89. Ape-shit, Basted, Boffed, Blind, Blitzkrieged, Blown Out, Brewed, Comatosed, Crispy, Faced (from Shit-faced), Farmed, Feeling No Pain, Gone, Got to Down, Hurtin'. Invertebrated, Juiced, Knee-walking, Laid Out, LD (from learning disabled), Legless, Lit, Looped, Messed Up, Nine-eyed, No Condition to be in the Public Eye, Obliterated, Otis, Out of Here, Paralytic, Pickled, Planted, Plastered, Ploughed, Polluted, Ripped, Ripped Out of One's Gourd, Ripped to the Tits, Saturated, Shit-faced, Slammed, Sloshed, Smashed, Smuckered, Snockered, Soused, Tanked, Ted (from Wasted), Tight as a Coot, Toasted, Totalled Out, Tore Out of the Frame, Trashed, Wasted, Whipped, Wide Open, Wiped Out, Woofy, Wrecked, Zooed, Zulued.

The action of imbibing alcohol has also spawned a variety of quasi-synonymous verbs. Many of those in use at North Carolina refer specifically to drinking beer.

Troll

Catch a Buzz, Crack Some Suds, Do 12 Oz. Curls, Kill a Few Brain Cells, Kill Some Gray Matter, Pop Tops, Pound a Few, Pull a Drunk, Quaff, Rally, Shoot a Beer, Sip Suds, Smoke a Ha, Suck Out a Few Heads, Troll (from the name of the local bar *Trolls*).

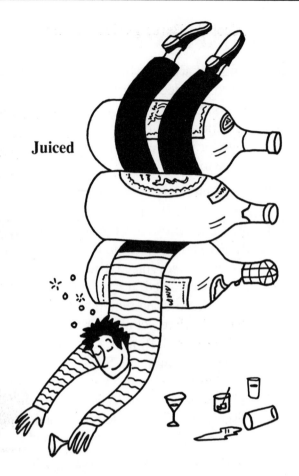

Juiced

Beer itself is called by a variety of names, several of which are formed on specific brand names.

Beast (Milwaukee's Best), Brew, Brewdog, Brewha, Brewski, Brewster, Budwiper, Chilly Dog, Cool Gut, Coolone, Corn Do-Do, Golden Nectar, Greenie Wienie (Heineken), Ha-Ha, Heinie (Heineken), Hummer, Joe (Schlitz, from the Joseph Smith Brewing Co.), Natty Bo (Natural Bohemian), Party-in-a-Can, Sauce, Silver Bullet (Coors Light), Tin, Twize (Budweiser).

A variety of other expressions also refer to the pastime of drinking.

AUNT BETSY'S COOKIE STORE   Alcoholic Beverage Control store.

BEER-GOGGLES, BEER-NOCULARS   Impaired vision brought on by drinking which makes members of the opposite sex look better. "Kevin must have had major *beergoggles* on last night because he kept hitting on the ugliest girl there."

EIGHTY-SIX   To stop serving someone alcohol because he or she is drunk. "The bartender *eighty-sixed* John after five drinks."

SHOTGUN   A method of drinking beer in which the can is turned upside down and punctured and then opened on the top by the tab so that the beer comes rushing out and has to be swallowed in rapid gulps. "They made pledges do *shotguns* with BEAST."

WASTE MACHINE, WASTE PRODUCT   Someone who has drunk too much.

Beer Goggles

COOKING THE BOOKS: Studying

Although taking courses and studying are supposedly the major activities of students, college slang does not reflect this. The work of studying and discussing studies is carried out in the standard language. However, attitudes and emotional reactions to studying are expressed in slang, with most of the slang expressions falling into a few categories of meaning.

Studying Hard:

Book, Book It, Burn, Burn the Midnight Oil, Bust Ass, Cook the Books, Crack a Book, Cram, Crank, Hit the Books, Kick Ass, Make Love to the Books, Pull an All-nighter, Rock the House, Rush the Attic.

One Who Studies Hard:

Eggbert, Egghead, Gunner, Merv, Pencil Neck, Poindexter, Study Dweeb.

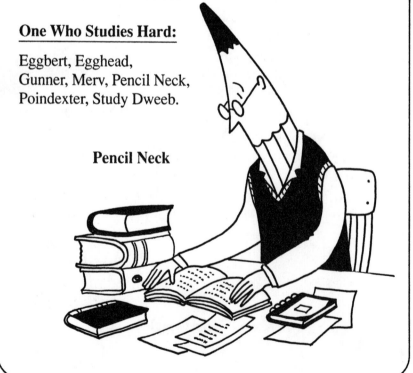

Pencil Neck

Failing to Attend Class:

Bag, Blow off, Cut, Ditch, Dust, Lay Out Of, Pull a Ferris Buhler, Punt.

An Easy Course:

Betty Crocker Course, Breeze, Crib Course, Crip Course, Football Course, Gravy, Piece of Cake, Skate, Slide, Sandbox 101, Moons for Goons (Astronomy), Polislide (Political Science), Rocks for Jocks (Geology).

GRADES	
A.	ACE, BLITZ, DO BONUS, KICK BUTT, SMOKE
B.	B-OUT
C.	HOOK, C YOUR WAY THROUGH
D.	DOG, DONUT
F.	BLOW, BOMB, BRICK, FLAG, GET SPANKED, PUNCH OUT, WAVE
ZOO.	To make the worst grade in the class
INK.	To make the grade *incomplete*

Miscellaneous:

CRISIS MODE In a panic, pressured by obligations. "I'm in *crisis mode* — three midterms and two papers this week."

THE MAGNET Whatever lures students away from their studies. "*The magnet* is turned on every Thursday night at 10 PM. There's nothing I can do about it."

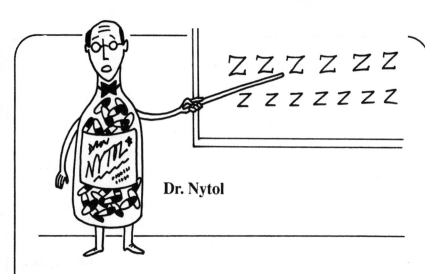

Dr. Nytol

MR. ROGERS A boring professor. Also DR. NYTOL.

SINGLE EXPOSURE Having read the material for a test only one time. "I went into that English 38 test *single exposure* and really bombed it."

SUCK WIND To speak in class unprepared; to embarrass one's self in class. "She called on me for an answer, and man, did I ever *suck wind*."

SUZIE SORORITY Typical sorority member. Also BUFFY, MUFFY, SORORITY SUE, SUE, SUZIE, SUZIE SORO.

GREEK SPEAK:
Sorority and Fraternity Life

The self-selecting social organizations which name themselves by Greek letters, like Tau Kappa Epsilon or Delta Delta Delta, are natural breeding grounds for slang on all campuses that have a Greek system. A constant preoccupation of fraternities and sororities is attracting and keeping suitable members, and many of the slang terms refer to various steps in this process. Some expressions are used nationally throughout the Greek System, while others are characteristic of one campus or one local chapter.

ALL CAMPUS Party held at a fraternity house to which everyone is welcome.

AX-QUEEN Sorority member who does not seem to like any rushees.

BAUNCH To eliminate a rushee from further consideration.

BUMP To circulate at a party in a pre-arranged system in order to replace another sorority member in a conversation with a rushee.

DIAMOND IN THE RUFF Rushee unknown to sorority members.

FRAT OUT To dress and act like a typical fraternity member.

FRATTY BAGGER A fraternity member. Also BAGGER, FRAT RAT.

G. D. I. Student who does not belong to a fraternity or sorority. From God Damned Independent.

Q. B. T. Good times of male bonding. From Quality Brother Time.

RHONDA RUSHEE Typical female who wishes to join a sorority.

RUSHEE Female student participating in the prescribed social activities preliminary to joining a sorority.

STRANGER Person met for the first time on a blind date, or STRANGER DATE.

SUICIDE For a rushee to write down one sorority only when designating her preferences.

V. N. B.   Bland, non-distinctive rushee. From *Very Nice But . . .*

WELL BRED BUT WELL FED   Overweight rushee.

YEA-RAH   Rushee known to sorority members before the period of rush. Also HOT RUSHEE, KEY RUSHEE.

CRANKING TUNES: Music

BEACH MUSIC   Music for dancing the SHAG.

BOOGIE   To dance. Also CUT THE RUG, GET OFF, GRIND, JAM, JUKE, RIP THE RUG.

Third World Briefcase

CRANK TUNES	To play music at a high volume.
DEADHEAD	A fan of the rock group The Grateful Dead.
DEAD VIRGIN	Someone unfamiliar with The Grateful Dead rock group.
DENTIST OFFICE MUSIC	Slow, boring, uninteresting song.
DRUG MUSIC	Any contemporary rock music characterized by highly repetitive chord progressions and vague lyrics about alienation and narcotics.
HEAD-BANGER	One who loves and always listens to hard rock music.
HOUSE MIX	The longer, specially recorded, disc jockey-manipulated versions of popular dance tunes heard at bars and clubs.
JAM	To play music. Also to KICK OUT SOME JAM.
JAMBOX	Large portable stereo radio and cassette player. Also BOX, BOOGIE BOX, GHETTO BLASTER, GHETTO BOX, GHETTO BUSTER, THIRD WORLD BRIEFCASE.
METAL HEAD	A person who enjoys listening to hard rock and heavy metal music.
SHAG	Popular dance similar to the jitterbug.
TUNES	Music of any kind.

Metal Head

RAGGING: Clothing

Bowhead

BOWHEAD Someone who wears large fashionable hair-bows; a typical sorority member. "Can you believe that geek is dating a *bowhead?*"

CAPTAIN HIPNESS Stylishly dressed male.

CONVALE-SCENT GOWN A matronly-looking dress.

DANGLING MODIFIER A single long, often flashy, earring.

EARTH MUFFIN Person who is out of style. Also called a GRANOLA.

FASHION POLICE Fashion conscious, stylishly dressed members of campus cliques. "The Hardback Cafe is usually filled with *fashion police.*"

FILE To dress up. From *profile.* Also STYLIN' AND PROFILIN'.

GO COMMANDO To go without underwear; to forget to pack underwear.

G. Q. Fashionably and tastefully dressed. Usually applies to males. From *Gentlemen's Quarterly.*

JESUS SANDALS Birkenstock Earth Sandals. "Everyone else in my Comp Lit course must be graduate students — they were all wearing *Jesus Sandals.*"

PREP OUT To wear an assemblage of certain name-brand clothing and jewelry associated with the preppy look.

RAG BACK To show off by dressing well and looking sophisticated.

RAG OUT To wear old, sloppy clothes.

RAGGING Well-dressed.

SHEET IT To wear a dress or skirt without stockings or socks, i.e., to have white legs. "Dr. Roth said that because the air conditioning is broken, she recommends *sheeting it* tomorrow."

Go Commando

TREND-INISTAS Political or social activists who combine heightened political consciousness with stylish clothing.

BLIMPING OUT: Eating

Eating Voraciously:

Blimp Out, Chow Down, Commit a Food Crime, Grease, Grease Down, Grind, Grub, Hone Out, Hoover, Meal, Mow Down, Munch Out, Narf, Pig Out, Pork Out, Scarf, Snort Out, Throw Down, Trough Out.

Blimp Boat

Person Who Has Eaten Too Much; An Overweight Person:

Blimp Boat, Bloater, Bus, Chubbo, Chubbo-twin, Candidate for Pigginess, Grit Packer, Hog, Lardass, Oinker, Pig Boat, Pig Dog, Porker, Ricer (on Rice Diet at Duke University), Whale.

GOOB-A-TRON:
The Social Outcast

The Big L, Corndog, Donut Crew, Dork, Dweeb, Dweebie, Elrod, Geek, Goob, Goober, Goob-a-tron, Goomer, Gooper, Gweeb, L7 (from the square shape of capital L and 7 side by side), Neomaxumzumdweebie, Nerd, Nob, Nothing Burger, Paste Eater, Quimp, Reeb, Scoob, Social Donut, Social Donut Hole, Social Zero, Three Dimensional Loser, Three Dollar Bill, Turkey, Twirp, Yernt, Zero.

VACANT LOT:
Out of Touch

Different from social outcasts, who have no redeeming social virtues, are those who are temporarily out of touch with reality, like *space cookies*, and those who were once in style, but have not conformed to more recent trends, like *soybean people*. Many slang expressions with the meaning out of touch with reality draw on images of air and space and are included in that category earlier in this book.

Unaware

Clueless, Ditzy, Doesn't Have Both Oars in the Water, Doing a Vanna White, Elevator Doesn't Go to the Top, Hasn't Checked In, In the Fog, In Orbit, In the Twilight Zone, Lost In the Ozone, Light's On But Nobody's Home, Lunchy, Not Wrapped Too Tight, On a Mission, One Brick Shy of a Load, O. T. L., Out to Lunch, Spaced Out, Spacey.

Someone Who is Unaware:

Dingbat, Ditzo, Lunchbox, Lunchsack, Jetson, Sergeant Space, Space Case, Space Cookie, Suzie Spaceship, UFO, Vacant Lot, Z-head.

Someone Who is Out of Date:

Boheme, Bohemian, Boho, Crunchy Granola, Earth Daddy, Earth Momma, Earth Muffin, Earthy-crunchy, Fern, Granola, Granola-ite, Grapenut, Groover, Heywow, Hippie, No Nuker, Soybean People, Square, Zod.

Vacant Lot

COLOR ME GONE: Leaving

Ankle Express, Blow This Joint, Bolt, Boogie, Book, Book It, Break Camp, Bun This J, Color Me Gone, Dodge, Get the Hell Out of Dodge, Haul Ass, Haul Buggy, Hoof It, Blow This Popsicle Stand, Blow this Taco Stand, Make Like a Baby and Head Out, Make Like a Tree and Leave, Matriculate, Motivate, Motorvate, Off Like a Prom Dress, Outta Here, Put It in the Wind, Put Wheels on It, Sko ("Let's go"), Slide, Split.

Blow This Taco Stand

TALKING TO RALPH: Vomiting

Campus party animals are familiar with the consequences of drinking too much and have developed a number of synonyms to describe their uncomfortable condition.

Barf, Blow Cookies, Blow Chunks, Blow Grits, Blow Lunch, Boot, Bow to the Porcelain God, Call Earl, Call Hughie, Daniel Boone Club (refers to someone who "Goes Out and Shoots his Lunch"), Drive the Porcelain Bus, Go to Europe with Ralph and Earl in a Buick, Hug the Throne, Laugh at

the Carpet, Lose Lunch, Lose One's Groceries, Marry Your
Porcelain Mistress, Pray to the Enamel God, Ralph, Sell
Buicks, Shoot Your Cookies, Spill the Blue Groceries, Spit
Beef, Spule, Talk into the Porcelain Telephone, Talk to Earl,
Talk to Ralph on the Big White Phone, Technicolor Yawn,
Throw Donuts, Toss Cookies, Toss Groceries, Toss One's
Tacos, Waste Groceries, Wheeze, Woof, Woof Cookies,
Worship the Porcelain Goddess, Worship the Throne.

SCOOPAGE:
The Opposite Sex

BAMA   Ugly female. Also BARFOLA, BAT, BOO-
             HOG, MUD PUPPY, PAPER BAG CASE
             ("She needs to wear one or more bags over
             her face."), DOUBLE BAGGER, TRIPLE
             BAGGER, SIX-PACK GIRL ("Her date has
             to drink a six-pack before he can look at her.")

FUTURE   Unattractive male.
             ("It will be a long
             time in the future
             before he looks good.")

HE COULD Exclamation of
MAKE ME   approval of a
WRITE   male's looks.
BAD
CHECKS!

GRASS-   Hometown
ROOTS   sweetheart.

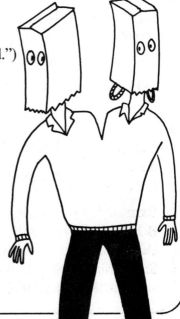

Double Bagger

79

HUNK	Handsome, well-built male. Also ADONIS, BEEF-A-RONI, BEEFCAKE, CRUSHMAN, DEMI-GOD, DROOL-OVER, FACEMAN, GREEK GOD, HUB, RESIDENT AREA GOD, TASTY BABE.
I. D.	Female with no career ambitions. From Industrial Debutante.
MERCY	Very beautiful and sexy woman. Also BRICK HOUSE, BURGER, DOUBLE BURGER, TRIPLE BURGER WITH CHEESE, FLY GIRL, HAMMER, STONE FOX.
NERD MAGNET	Female who seems to attract NERDS.
NICE CAR	Attractive male or female.
PHAT	Having a shapely body, applied to females. Popularly supposed from Pretty Hips And Thighs.
SCOOPAGE	Potential date material.
SCRUMP QUEEN	Promiscuous female. Also HOSEBAG, RACK-DATE, ROAD WHORE, SLEAZEBAG, SLEAZEBUCKET, TRIM.
STUD	A macho male. Also GUIDO.

IN CRUISE MODE:
Looking for Ms./Mr. Right

Looking

Check the Block, Cruise, Do the Street, Give Someone the Cyclops, Go for the Cheese, Lock It in Cruise Mode, Put It in Cruise Mode, Put It into Overdrive, Scope, Take in the Sights, Troll, 12:00 High-check It Out

Trying to Seduce:

Crack On, Go for It, Hit On, Put the Rush On, Put the Move On, Scam On, Skeem On, Work It.

MAJOR MAKE-OUT SCENE: Sex

Kissing:

Box Tonsils, Eat Face, Face-rape, Give a Tonsilectomy, Go for Sushi (deep kissing), Grub, Mesh, M. L. A. (Massive Lip Action), Mug, Munch out, Play Tonsil Hockey, Scooch, Some Smacky, Smooch, Suck Heads.

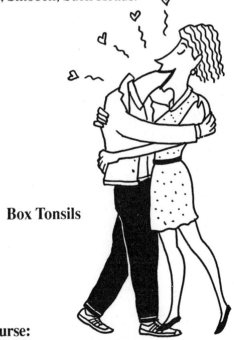

Box Tonsils

Intercourse:

Bone Dance, Bop, Bounce Refrigerators, Do Night Laps, Do the Funky Alphonso, Do the Nasty, Get Down to Basics, Horizontal Bop, Horizontal Mambo, Horizontal Twist and Shout, Parallel Park, The Ootie Ootie, Scrog, Scrump, Slam, Sling Up With

Later, Later Tater

WHAT'S GOING DOWN?:
Hello and Goodby

Hello:

Check In, How Do?, How's It Happening?, Sup?, What Does It Look Like?, What It Is?, What's Going Down?, What's Happening?. What's Jumping?, What's Shaking?, What's the Deal?, What's Up?, What You Know?, Yo.

Goodby:

Catch You Later, Catch You on the Flip Flop, Check You, Check You on the Flip Side, G. B., Gotta Slide, I'm Art, I'm Archives, I'm History, It's Been Real, Later, Later Tater, Lasta On, Outta Here, See You on the Rebound, Sko.

TARHEEL TURF:
Local College Slang

Although much college slang travels quickly from campus to campus and constitutes an ever-changing and amorphous body of general college slang, students at every college and university develop expressions pertinent to their own locale

— for example, names for buildings, courses, and social activities. Those developed at the University of North Carolina differ in particular but not in kind from those developed on other college campuses; for instance, every group of college students creates unfavorable nicknames for the cafeteria and for nearby schools.

ARB OUT To relax in Coker Arboretum.

THE BEACH The grassy area in front of Connor Dorm. Also CONNOR BEACH.

B. K. LOUNGE Burger King. Also DINE WITH ROYALTY.

BO-BORO Nearby Carrboro, N.C.

BURNOUT Annual, outdoor, open campus party to benefit the N. C. Jaycees' Burn Center.

CHANCE CAFETERIA Chase cafeteria.

THE CONVENT Spencer Residence Hall. Also SPINSTER DORM.

THE DEAN DOME The Dean E. Smith Student Activities Center.

DOOKIE Student at Duke University.

D. U. M. B. Duke University Marching Band.

D. U. M. B.

EARL-BURGER Cheeseburger served every Friday night at the Kappa Alpha house. Named after their cook, Earl D. Woods.

E-HAUS Ehringhaus Residence Hall.

FAYETTE-NAM	Fayetteville, N. C., home of Fort Bragg and the Green Berets. Also FEDVILLE.
GRAN-VILE	Granville Towers Residence Hall. Also GROSS-VILLE and GROSS-VILE TOWERS.
HILTON JAMES	Hinton James Residence Hall.
H-STREET	Henderson St. Bar.
JOCK WALL	Wall in front of Greenlaw Hall where the athletes hang out between classes.
LENWAH	Lenoir Cafeteria.
MAC'S SUPPER CLUB	McDonald's
THE ONION	The Student Union.
THE OVERGRAD	The Wilson, and, now, Davis Library.
PARKER RUN	Quick trip to the nearest dormitory that houses vending machines with junk food. Originated in Avery Dorm.
THE PIT	The open, bricked area between Student Stores, the Union, and Lenoir.
PIT PREACHERS	Christian evangelists who regularly proselytize in The Pit.
RUMPTY-VUMP	R. T. V. M. P. The Department of Radio-Television-Motion Pictures.
SLIME ROOM	The old Pine Room cafeteria in the basement of Lenoir. Also SWINE ROOM.
SPANKIT	To go to Spanky's Restaurant.

Mac's Supper Club

STUDENT DEATH Student Health Services.

THE UGLY The Robert B. House Undergraduate Library. Also U. L., THE ZOO.

UNIVERSITY OF NEW JERSEY AT DURHAM Duke University.

U. N. C. AT HARDEE'S The University of North Carolina at Wilmington. Also U. N. C. AT K-MART.

U. N. C. AT TWEETSIE RAILROAD Appalachian State University in Boone, N. C.

THE YARD The area from Polk Place to The Pit.

Brick

B-BALL: Sports

Because athletic activities provide the opportunity for a great amount of social life on college campuses, sports serve as natural subject matter for the proliferation of college slang. Much sports slang used on college campuses is not collegiate at all but comes from radio and television announcers. Although the University of North Carolina fields twenty-six intercollegiate athletic teams, basketball is the premiere sport and the inspiration for most Carolina sports slang.

AIR　　To jump high as prelude to slam-dunking a basketball. Also SKY.

B-BALL　　Basketball. Also THE PILL, ROUNDBALL.

BOTTOM!　　Expression of approval for a beautiful shot.

BREATHER U.　　A college whose basketball team is not highly rated. "Carolina played a bunch of *Breather U.'s* over Christmas, so of course they won."

BRICK　　A poor shot in basketball, usually off the rim. "Jeff's game is really off — he just shot another *brick*."

HAWK SOME BALL	To play a recreational game of basketball.
JAMBURGER CITY!	Exclamation following a crowd-pleasing dunk.
J	Jump shot.
LONG DISTANCE DEDICATION	Basketball shot from more than twenty feet.
PUMP 'EM IN	To make many baskets. "Lebo really *pumped 'em in* at the end of the game."
RAIN- MAKER	Basketball shot with a high arc, usually shot from a long distance.
SHOOT SOME HOOP	To shoot baskets or play a pickup game. Also SHOOT THE PILL, SHOOT THE ROCK, POUND THE ROCK.
SHOOT THE EYES OUT OF IT	To shoot the basketball extremely well.
SWISHER	A shot that goes in without touching the rim.
TREY	A three-point shot.

Playing Well or Winning:

Abuse, Another One Bites the Dust, Burn, Deal, Dominate, Face, Jam On, Live On, School, Scold, Smoke, Use, Walk 'em Down, Wax, Whale On, Womp.

Playing Poorly or Losing:

Bite the Big One, Bite the Dust, Blow It, Bomb, Take the Gas, Get Blown Out, Get Creamed, Get Dogged, Get Piped, Get Rocked, Get Spanked, Get Used.

A MISCELLANY FROM HELL

ATTITUDE ADJUSTMENT HOUR Happy hour after work or classes.

Cog-D

CLUE BUS Reality. "Catch the *clue bus*. The all-campus is next weekend, not tomorrow."

COOL POINTS Imaginary system of points based on the sophistication of one's actions. "Mike suffered a major loss of *cool points* when he called his date the wrong name."

COG-D Muscular, solidly built.

COP A TUDE To have a bad attitude. "If you're going to *cop a tude* because I was a few minutes late, then I'll just go home."

COWBOY QUESTION A dare. "Jump the median — it's a *cowboy question*."

CRUMB To feel sad or depressed. "I've been *crumbing* all day about my grade in English 38."

FIVE-FINGER DISCOUNT To steal, shoplift. "Somebody put the *five-finger discount* on my I. D."

FROM HELL Very good or very bad. "We were ushers *from hell*. Nobody smoked in our section." "When it rains, I look like the reject French poodle queen *from hell*."

GET A JOB Stop annoying. "Would you *get a job* for a while — I'm trying to study."

INTELLEC-TUAL HOUR Time of day when cartoons are on television.

Five Finger Discount

MISS THING   Sarcastic noun of address among friends. "*Miss Thing*, wear those black boots. Just stop asking me how they look."

MY BAD   My fault, cause of misunderstanding. "I thought the film started at 9:15 — *my bad*." Also MY BURST, MY BUST.

ON-LINE   Technologically sophisticated or knowledgeable. "Hey, I've got a cellular with call-waiting. I'm *on-line*, pal."

SCHMIELAGE   Group of females.

Schmielage

SLAMMIN' JAMMIN' THROW DOWN HAPPY FEET   Exclamation of sheer joy. "This key lime pie is *slammin' jammin' throw down happy feet*."

THE STUDS	Arrogance. "He's got *the studs* since he made the football team."
TRIP	Exciting, stimulating. "Dr. Hall's lecture on Sonnet 35 was a *trip*."
TRIAL SIZE	Small, refers to a person. "It's a wonder that Karen is so tall. Her parents are *trial size*."
WEDGY	Underwear pulled up tight from the back by some-one else as a prank. "He gave me a *wedgy* so hard that the waistband ripped off my underwear."
WIPE ONE'S MOUTH	To finish. "I *wiped my mouth* on that, and I have nothing else to say."
YOU SHOT WHO?	"Say that again?" X: "Your share of the phone bill is $528." Y: "*You shot who?*"

QUIZ: Comprehensive

Match letters on right to numbers on left.

1. **AUNT BETSY'S COOKIE STORE**	A. **Food**
2. **BUEL**	B. **Excellent**
3. **BOGART**	C. **Out of fashion**
4. **GO FOR SUSHI**	D. **Take an unfair share**
5. **GRANOLA**	E. **Drunk**
6. **MY FEET ARE STAYING**	F. **Kiss passionately**
7. **FIVE-FINGER DISCOUNT**	G. **Steal**
8. **TECHNICOLOR YAWN**	H. **Liquor store**
9. **TED**	I. **Regurgitation**
10. **TUBULAR**	J. **Goodby**

Answers: 1 H; 2 A; 3 D; 4 F; 5 C; 6 J; 7 G; 8 I; 9 E; 10 B

College Slang 101

IV. WHY COLLEGE STUDENTS USE SLANG:
Value Judgments Without Commitment

Use of current slang by college students is a sign of social awareness and an acknowledgment of the importance of relationships with others. Slang provides college students with automatic affirmative and negative verbal responses for typical situations with peers, allowing the users to appear to make value judgments without actually taking a stand or exposing their feelings. Slang provides the words to soothe, commiserate, and encourage in the bad times, and to affirm, approve, and tease in the good times.

AWESOME VS. CHEEZY:
Evaluative Words

Positive:

Awesome, Bonus, Casual, Core, Daddy, Def, Electric, Fly, Fresh, Hardcore, Key, Killer, On, On the One, Organic, Primo, Smooth, Smoove, Stellar, Summit, Sweet.

Negative:

Budget, Buggy, Bush, Cheezy, Cheezy Sleazy Greasy, Crappy, Dip-Shitty, Dook, Doy, Generic, Gnarley, Gross, Heinous, Lame, Lowrent, Nappy, Pice, Rank.

BITE MOOSE: Retorts

Despite the abusiveness of many retorts in college slang, most of which are in the form of commands, such expressions are used mainly among friends and are understood to convey only temporary ill will. Often they are used in trivial situations in which the retort is understood to be an exaggeration.

BITE MOOSE   Go to hell. Also BITE OFF, FORGET YOU, GET BENT.

Bite Moose

CHILL OUT   Relax. Also COOL IT, COOL YOUR JETS, TAKE A CHILL PILL.

CUT ME SOME SLACK   Stop pressuring me. Also GET OFF MY CASE, GET OUT OF TOWN, GIVE ME A BREAK, LAY OFF.

GAG   That's disgusting. Also GAG ME WITH A SPOON, GAG ME WITH A SNOW SHOVEL.

GET A CLUE   Pay attention to what is important. Also GET A JOB, GET A LIFE, GET A REAL LIFE, GET WITH THE PROGRAM.

NS₂   Too bad. (*No Shit Sherlock.*)

WORD UP:
Agreement and Support

Expressions of encouragement and support are more varied
than are retorts. Sometimes an evaluative adjective like
awesome or *cool* is simply injected as affirmative feedback in
a conversation. Other expressions use the first person pronoun
I. As with many other slang items, specific meaning is derived
in large part from context and the tone of voice.

AIN'T LIFE A GRIN? I'm sorry this bad thing happened. Also DAMN A BEAR, DAMN A POLAR BEAR, I HATE IT, I HATE IT FOR YOU, SHIT HAPPENS, THAT BITES, THAT BITES THE BIG ONE.

DECENT That's great for you. Also AWESOME, JAMMING, and many other adjectives.

FOR SURE I agree. Also I'M THERE, I'M SERIOUS, REALLY, SOLID, WORD, WORD UP.

GO FOR IT I encourage you in this. Also DEAL, GET DOWN, RIGHT ON.

Published by Spectacle Lane Press